HOW TO BE AN ACTOR

AND OTHER FILM AND TV JOBS

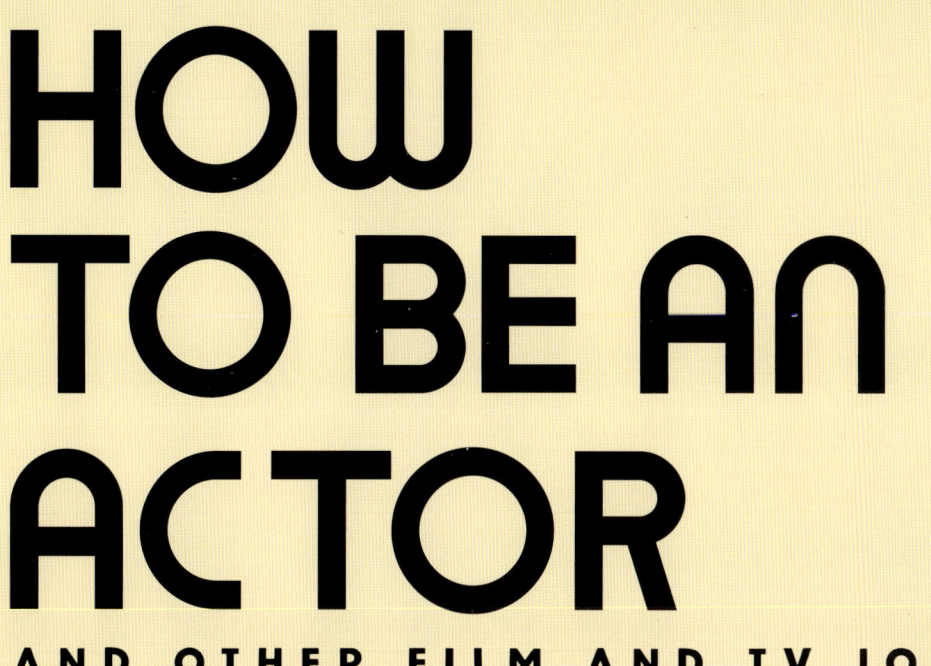

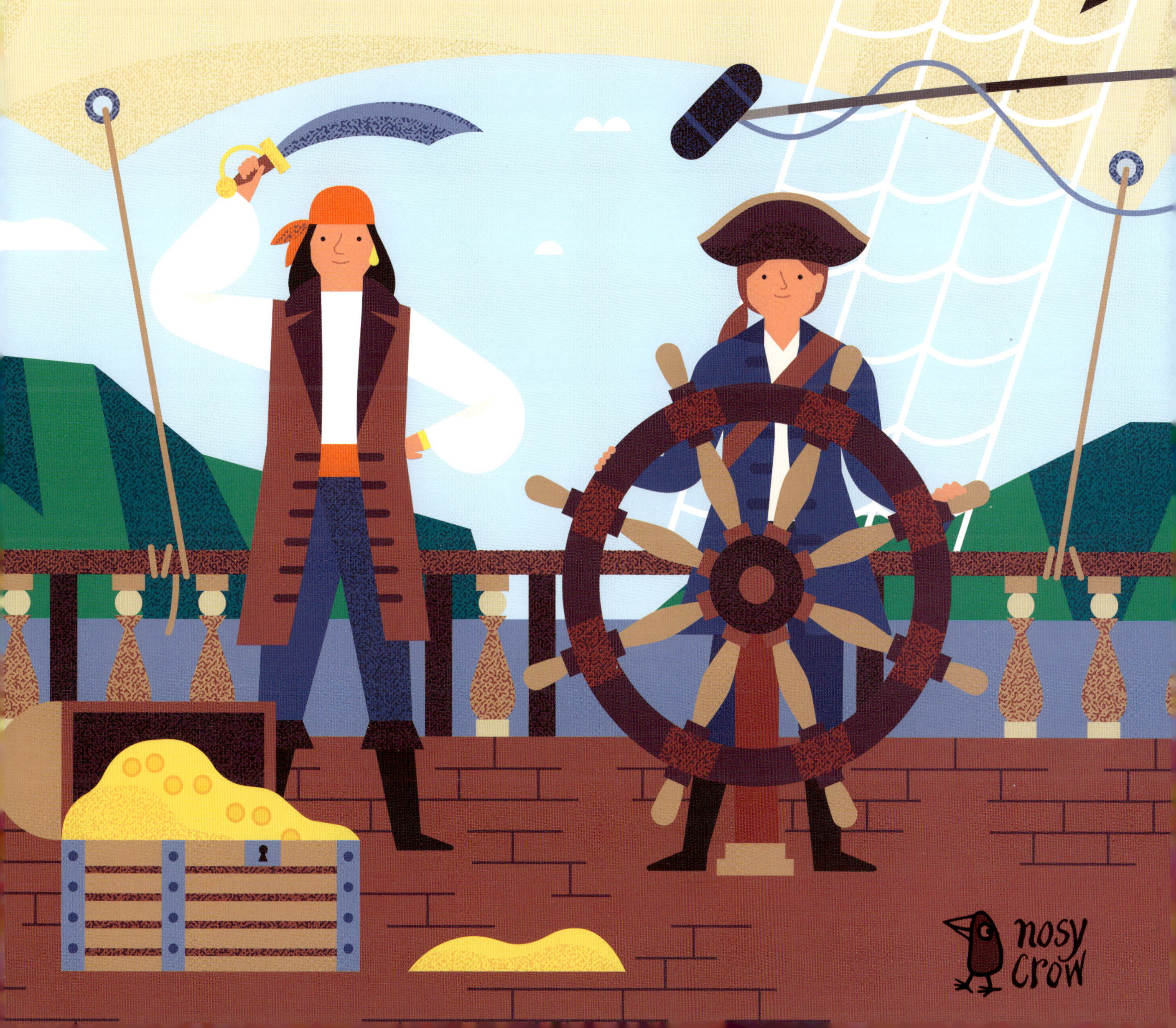

To all the wonderful wildlings in my life, especially Esti... May your imagination always be free and your stories find a way to be told. I love you! X
H.N.

To Belén, the most wonderful friend and actress there is. Love you always.
S.L.

First published 2025 by Nosy Crow Ltd
Wheat Wharf, 27a Shad Thames, London, SE1 2XZ, UK

Nosy Crow Eireann Ltd
44 Orchard Grove, Kenmare, Co Kerry, V93 FY22, Ireland

www.nosycrow.com

ISBN 978 1 83994 964 7 (HB)
ISBN 978 1 83994 965 4 (PB)

Nosy Crow and associated logos are trademarks and/or registered trademarks of Nosy Crow Ltd

Text © Hannah New 2025
Illustrations © Sol Linero 2025

The right of Hannah New to be identified as the author and Sol Linero to be identified as the illustrator of this work has been asserted.

All rights reserved.

This book is sold subject to the condition that it shall not, by way of trade or otherwise, be lent, hired out or otherwise circulated in any form of binding or cover other than that in which it is published. No part of this publication may be reproduced, stored in a retrieval system, or transmitted in any form or by any means (electronic, mechanical, photocopying, recording or otherwise) without the prior written permission of Nosy Crow Ltd.

The publisher and copyright holders prohibit the use of either text or illustrations to develop any generative machine learning artificial intelligence (AI) models or related technologies.

A CIP catalogue record for this book is available from the British Library.

Printed in China following rigorous ethical sourcing standards.

10 9 8 7 6 5 4 3 2 1 (HB)
10 9 8 7 6 5 4 3 2 1 (PB)

CONTENTS

WHAT IS AN ACTOR?	4
WHY DO WE NEED ACTORS?	6
THE HISTORY OF ACTING, FILM AND TV	8
HOW DO YOU BECOME AN ACTOR?	10
WHAT SKILLS DOES AN ACTOR NEED?	12
HOW DOES AN ACTOR GET A ROLE?	14
WHAT IS AN ACTOR'S DAY LIKE ON SET?	16
WHAT OTHER FILM AND TV JOBS ARE THERE?	18
ARE YOU GOOD AT PLANNING AND ORGANISATION? THEN A JOB IN PRODUCTION MANAGEMENT MIGHT BE FOR YOU	20
DO YOU LIKE FASHION, ART OR DESIGN? THEN TRY ONE OF THESE JOBS	22
DO YOU LOVE CAMERAS AND TECHNOLOGY? TRY A JOB IN THE TECHNICAL DEPARTMENT	24
WHAT ABOUT A JOB IN THE STUNT DEPARTMENT?	26
HOW IS A FILM OR TV SHOW EDITED?	28
WHAT ABOUT THE MORE UNUSUAL FILM AND TV JOBS?	30
GET INVOLVED!	32

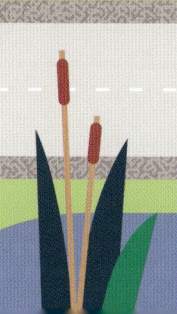

WHAT IS AN ACTOR?

An actor is someone who brings a character to life in a performance, using their body, voice and imagination.

The character might be a real person, a fictional person, or even an animal or fantasy creature. By speaking in a different accent or tone, changing their walk and using different body gestures or facial expressions, they can transform into these different characters and tell their stories.

Actors work alongside many other people, such as . . .

costume designers

make-up artists

light technicians

Actors can work in many different places, from theatres and film studios to museums, cruise ships and even theme parks. When the story is set in the past, they might have to perform in a castle or large old house, or if it is set in a particular climate they may travel to a jungle, beach, desert or snowy mountain.

directors and camera operators.

DID YOU KNOW?
You can act at any age. The oldest actor to appear in a film was 114 years old!

WHY DO WE NEED ACTORS?

Watching films and TV shows is fun, but why do we actually *need* actors?

Acting and storytelling has been used throughout history to talk about how people should behave in the world and to **ask big questions** about life. It can be a way to pass on **important information** through generations, especially in societies without written language.

Watching stories being told can bring communities together through the emotions that the audience experience, whether that's

joy and laughter in **feel-good films** and **comedies** . . .

or sadness and grief in **tragedies** or **dramas.**

Stories can also make people **see what life is like** for someone who may be very different from themselves. Actors can tell stories of people who come from **different backgrounds and cultures,** or who **think and feel differently.**

DID YOU KNOW?
There are hundreds of film and TV industries around the world, each with their own unique cultures and traits.

Actors in films, TV shows and theatre can help us understand what it feels like to be in another person's shoes, so that we can become a kinder and more inclusive society.

THE HISTORY OF
ACTING, FILM AND TV

We know from ancient African masks and records of mime, dance and puppetry in Asia that people have been performing for thousands of years.

The first written account of an actor was in ancient Greece. He was called Thespis. Today, 'thespian' is another name for an actor.

Performances became very popular and theatres such as The Globe in London, UK could hold up to 3,000 people.

Thomas Edison and William Dickson revealed the first film projector known as the 'Kinetoscope'.

| 560 BCE | 613 CE | 1600s | 1833 | 1890 | 1895 |

In China, the first known acting school was opened by Emperor Minghuang, in his pear garden.

William George Horner created the 'zoetrope', a cylinder with 12 images inside. When it was spun, it looked like the images were moving.

The Lumière Brothers held the first public film screening in Paris. They showed a series of black-and-white silent short films, accompanied by live music.

DID YOU KNOW?
The first Academy Awards (the Oscars) ceremony was held in 1929.

VHS 'videos' were invented in Japan so films could be played on people's TVs at home.

The 'Technicolor' process was invented which allowed people to film in colour, but it was not widely used until the 1930s. One of the first movies to use this process was *The Wizard of Oz* in 1939.

Cinema's 'Golden Age' began, when films were made with sound and colour. Many beautiful cinemas were built around the world, some of which could hold over 3,000 people.

| 1915 | 1926 | 1930s | 1940s | 1976 | 1980s |

John Logie Baird, a Scottish engineer, invented the first television set known as the 'Televisor'.

After the Second World War, a lot of people bought televisions and more TV shows were created, including the first children's programmes.

Films began to be edited digitally, and special effects became better and better!

9

HOW DO YOU BECOME AN ACTOR?

There are many different paths to becoming an actor, and it's never too early to start!

You can **join a local theatre or drama group.** Many schools, local youth centres and national youth organisations will have a group that you can join. They can help you learn acting, singing and dancing skills as well as what it means to work as a team to tell a story.

You can **watch great actors performing** on stage, on TV or in the cinema. As you watch, ask yourself what they are doing to make you like or dislike a character, and how they make you feel.

You can **read scripts and plays.** Plays are a great way to understand how a story is put together and can be told on stage.

You can **make your own plays or films.** Why not put on a show or film screening for your family and friends? It's a great way to learn about how to position actors and props, use a camera and edit a film.

DID YOU KNOW?
You don't need to go out and buy expensive camera equipment to make your own film. You can use any phone with a video camera!

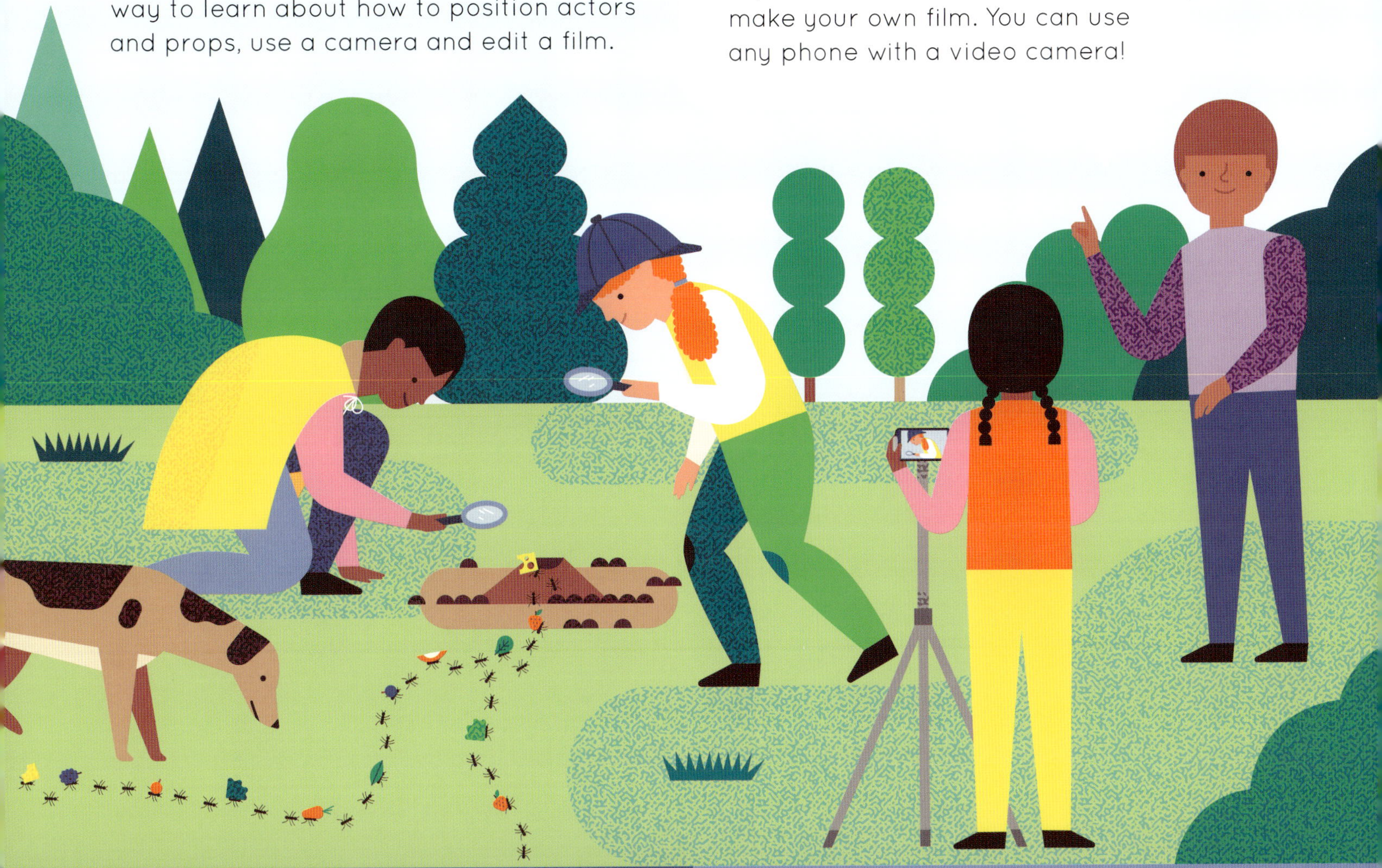

When you are old enough (around 18 years old), you can **apply to a drama school** to train as an actor. Usually, you have to audition to get a place at drama school – if you don't get in the first time, you can always try again.

But this is not the only way to start your acting career. Some actors work as a **supporting artist,** or **extra,** in crowd scenes. Or they might volunteer as an **assistant** on student productions, or take an **acting course.** The more **life experience** you gain, the wider range of roles you will be able to play.

WHAT SKILLS DOES AN ACTOR NEED?

As an actor, your tools are your mind, body and voice. You can learn to use these tools at any age and you will keep getting better the more you practise using them.

An actor will ask themselves what a character's **voice** sounds like. They'll think about what the character's childhood was like, where they grew up and moments in their life that might have shaped them.

They can then make decisions about the character's accent, rhythm of speech and the volume of their voice. They might even work with a **voice coach** to train for a role.

The way we move our bodies, or our **body language,** helps us communicate. Actors think very carefully about the character's way of moving. They may ask themselves questions like:

How does a confident, sad or excited person move?

What do they do for work that might affect how they move?

Are there any things that happened in the past that affect how they move?

Actors need to learn all their lines by heart, which can take a long time. To help with this, they train hard to improve their memory.

DID YOU KNOW?
Actors who work in musical theatre or musical films need to be good at singing and dancing.

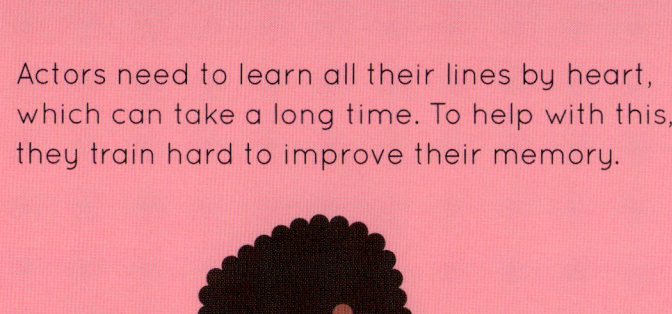

Sometimes an actor will need to learn about another country or time period to play their role. They might even have to **learn new skills,** such as horse-riding, playing an instrument, cooking, learning a new language, scuba-diving or martial arts.

To become an actor, it's important to be good at **receiving feedback from others,** as well as **communicating clearly** and **working well in a team.** Sometimes an actor will need to improvise if something goes wrong on set, so it is helpful to have a **good imagination** and an **open mind!**

HOW DOES AN ACTOR GET A ROLE?

Many actors start their careers by performing in small theatre shows or short films made by students. To get bigger roles, most actors will find an agent or a manager.

Agents help actors to find jobs, while **managers** help the actor with daily tasks and advise them on the types of jobs that will move their career forward. Both agents and managers work together to ensure that the actor is treated fairly.

DID YOU KNOW?
Actors might invite agents to performances of their plays or send them a **showreel** – clips of the actor performing, edited together.

Agents are usually the first to hear about new roles. If they feel a role is right for one of their actors, they will send the actor's details to the **casting director,** who is in charge of finding actors for films and TV shows. The actor might then be asked to **audition** for the role.

The first round of auditions are usually done by **self-tape,** where the actor will record a scene themselves at home or in a studio. The casting director watches all the tapes sent in for each role and draws up a shortlist of actors they think might be right for the role.

They may offer the role to an actor straight away, or they might invite them to a **recall** or **call-back audition.** This could be another self-tape, or an audition in the casting director's office.

Sometimes directors will hold an in-person audition called a **chemistry read** to check whether two or more actors work well together.

You won't get every role you audition for. Most actors audition for many different roles before they get a job. The important thing is to **learn** from every audition, **stay positive, keep trying** and most of all **have fun** creating characters!

15

WHAT IS AN ACTOR'S DAY LIKE ON SET?

Days on set can be very long with a lot of waiting around, but they are also very exciting! Here is what a typical day might look like . . .

6am: Arrive on set for 'call time'
You will be taken to your trailer or green room, where you can stretch, do a little voice warm-up, and look over the **call-sheet** (schedule) and **sides** (pages of the script) for the day.

6.30am: Hair and make-up
The hair and make-up artists will start to transform you into your character.

7.45am: Put on your costume
After a quick breakfast, your dresser will help you put your costume on. Someone from the sound department might place a microphone on you.

8.30am: Rehearsal/blocking
The director will ask you to read through the scene with the other actors and talk about how you will move around during the scene.

8.45am: Crew show
The crew will watch a rehearsal (practice performance) of the scene. **Stand-ins** (people who look similar to the actors) will then be asked to stand in position and the actors can go back to their green room while the camera and lighting departments set up everything they need for that shot.

9am: Lights, camera, action!
Usually, a scene will be shot from different angles and with various light set-ups. You may be shooting that one scene all day or for several days! Or you might have to change costume and travel to a different location to shoot other scenes.

1pm: Cut!
Time to break for lunch, as well as hair-and-make-up retouches.

2pm: Back to set
You will be taken back to set and the filming can continue.

6pm: That's a wrap!
After finishing, or **wrapping,** on set you will be helped out of your costume and taken to hair and make-up to **de-rig,** which is where any make-up, hairstyles or wigs will be removed before you go home.

WHAT OTHER FILM AND TV JOBS ARE THERE?

Have you ever wondered who comes up with the idea for a film or TV show? Many people are involved in turning an idea into a script, and they are all part of the development team.

Screenwriters write scripts, also known as screenplays, either from their own ideas or ideas that have been given to them by a producer.

Commissioners work for a TV channel and decide which scripts will be given the money to be made.

Producers are the overall decision makers. They come up with story ideas, find the screenwriters, decide how much money the show or film will have and make sure all the departments are happy. They need a whole team of people to help them!

Directors are in charge on set. Their job is to make sure they get the best performance from the actors and that the scenes are shot perfectly. Directors work closely with all departments, from the screenwriters to the producers.

Casting directors work closely with the producers and directors to find the perfect actors for each role in the script. They are helped by **casting assistants,** who also do tasks in the office such as answering phones.

DID YOU KNOW?
Some films or TV shows are book adaptations – books that are turned into screenplays with permission from the authors.

Development researchers come up with new ideas for TV shows. They are always on the lookout for the most interesting subjects, places and people.

ARE YOU GOOD AT PLANNING AND ORGANISATION?
THEN A JOB IN PRODUCTION MANAGEMENT MIGHT BE FOR YOU.

Assistant directors help and support the director by planning the filming schedule. They think carefully about all the scenes that must be shot and where, which roles they include, how long they will take and all the equipment and teams that will need to be involved.

DID YOU KNOW?
Transport captains organise all the cars and drivers for the cast to get to set, and buses needed for extras.

Line producers are in charge of hiring and communicating with the crew. They make sure the project is running safely, on time and within budget (plan for how much money to spend on the project).

Locations managers find the best places for filming, from creaky old houses to wild woodlands. They have to get permission to temporarily close roads and make sure that nearby wildlife isn't disturbed.

Production coordinators create all the call-sheets (schedules) and sides (pages of the script), and make sure they are sent to everyone. After the day's filming is done, they will send progress reports (updates) to the director and producers.

Production accountants work with the producers to manage payments. They make sure that everyone is getting paid the right amount and that the final cost of the film or show doesn't go 'over budget' (when too much money is spent).

Most people who want to work in production start off as a **runner**. **Floor runners** run various errands, pass on messages between departments, and make sure that everyone is in the right place at the right time. **Production runners** complete office tasks like sharing the call-sheets and sides, answering the phone and organising paperwork.

DO YOU LIKE FASHION, ART OR DESIGN?
THEN TRY ONE OF THESE JOBS.

From tiaras to top hats, and wardrobes to wallpaper, a lot of thought goes into what each character and scene looks like ...

Costume designers come up with costumes for each character. They draw sketches and create 'mood boards' before finding **pattern cutters, seamstresses** and **jewellers** to make the costumes.

Dressers help the actors get into their costumes. They are often on set to check the costumes look good and don't get damaged, wrinkled or stained during filming.

Hair and make-up designers design each character's hairstyle and make-up look. They hire a team of **make-up artists, hairdressers** and **wigmakers** who have the skills to create their designs.

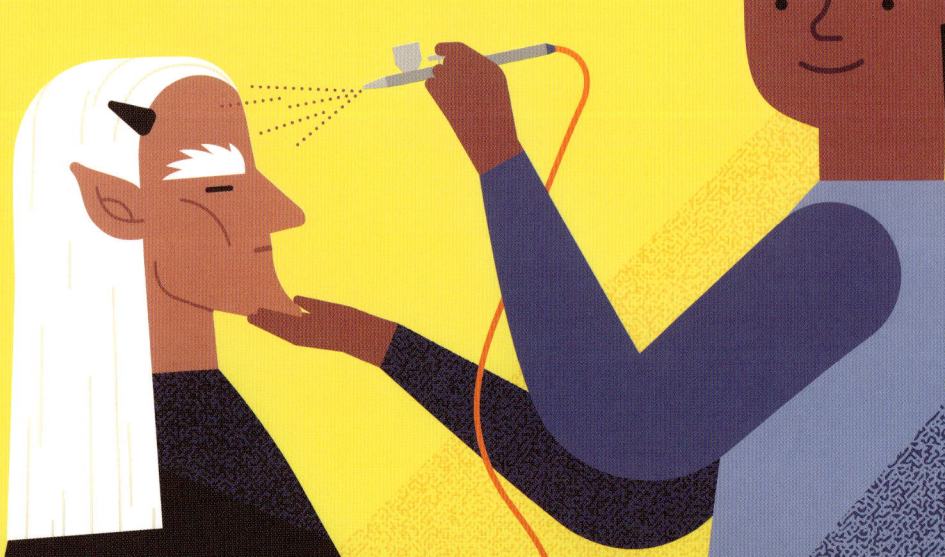

DID YOU KNOW?
Make-up artists can change the shape of an actor's face or make them look different with **prosthetics,** a special material stuck on to the actor's face, covered with make-up.

Construction managers build the sets with the help of carpenters, builders and painters. They make sure everything is done in a safe and environmentally friendly way.

Set designers know how to build houses and other structures that look real but are not.

Set decorators find all the furniture for the set. They sometimes work with the visual effects teams to create certain environments, such as a rose garden in winter or a ski slope in summer!

Prop masters make, buy, organise and transport all the props needed for each scene.

Production designers think carefully about what the film or TV show will look like, whether that's brightly coloured or gritty and dark, futuristic or set in the past.

Art directors make sure the production designer's vision can be achieved. They have a lot of technical knowledge and usually hire a big team of craftspeople to help make everything they need.

23

DO YOU LOVE CAMERAS AND TECHNOLOGY?
TRY A JOB IN THE TECHNICAL DEPARTMENT.

The technical department is in charge of everything from the cameras to the sound and lighting.

Directors of photography (DoPs) work closely with directors to make sure the scenes are captured perfectly. They decide which camera, lens, amount of lighting and camera movement are needed.

Grips are in charge of all the equipment needed to support the cameras, such as tripods, cranes, dollies (tripods on wheels), gimbles (which keep cameras steady when moving) and Steadicams (which keep cameras worn by operators steady and comfortable).

Digital imaging technicians (DITs) advise the DoP on the best settings for the camera and check what has been shot after each take.

Focus pullers or 1st assistant cameras (1st ACs) make sure the person or object being filmed is kept in focus (doesn't look fuzzy).

Camera operators capture, or 'shoot', the film or TV show, following instructions from the DoP on how to set up the shot.

Sound mixers make sure everything you can hear, from speech to special effects, is recorded properly.

Boom operators use a microphone on a long pole known as a 'boom' to record what the actors are saying.

Radio mic operators are in charge of the small microphones worn by the actors under their clothing.

DID YOU KNOW?
The clapperboard is used to mark which scene, take and sequence (section of a scene) is being shot to make everything clear when it's being edited.

Clapperboard operators or 2nd assistant cameras (2nd ACs) set up and test the cameras, check the batteries are charged and mark the actors' positions on the floor. When filming begins, they stand in front of the camera with a clapperboard before the director calls, "Action!"

Gaffers create and control the lighting set-up for each shot.

Lighting trainees unload the lighting equipment from the van and organise all the different filters and gels (coloured see-through plastic that change the colour of a light).

25

WHAT ABOUT A JOB IN THE STUNT DEPARTMENT?

Have you ever seen an explosion, crash or fight in a film or TV show? These were created with the hard work of the stunt department.

Some actors perform stunts themselves. But if the scene is too dangerous or difficult, a **stunt double** will do it instead. They look similar to the actor and are often highly skilled in martial arts, gymnastics, rally-car driving and more.

DID YOU KNOW?
If a very specific skill is needed, such as skiing, surfing, sky-diving or climbing, a sports champion might be called in for some scenes.

A team of **medics** or **first-aiders** are always on hand in case a stunt goes wrong and the actor injures themselves.

Stunt coordinators are in charge of the whole stunt department. They plan how the stunts will work, make sure they will be done safely and find the stunt double to perform them.

Fight coordinators and choreographers work with the actors and stunt doubles to create all the different movements of a fight.

Special equipment is needed for flying scenes.
Wire riggers help actors and stunt doubles into harnesses and attach them to wires, which are lifted up by cranes.

Sometimes actors are lifted by robotic arms or equipment called 'tuning forks', which are attached to their hips. Or they might be put in a wind tunnel, so it looks like they are falling from the sky.

If guns or explosives are involved, a **special effects** team will work with the actor to show them what they must do to make the explosion or gun fight look real and ensure that particular sequence can be performed safely.

HOW IS A FILM OR TV SHOW EDITED?

Post-production is when the film or TV show is edited and the film comes to life! This is when music, sound, graphics, visual effects and CGI (computer generated imagery) are added.

The **editor** cuts and combines the footage using a special computer program. They work closely with the director to ensure that the final footage is achieving the director's vision.

ADR (additional dialogue recording) editors record the actor reading lines that were not captured properly on set or that happen off-screen.

Foley artists create sound effects like footsteps or doors slamming. They have special tricks for recording difficult sounds – such as snapping celery to mimic the sound of broken bones!

Music composers write the music for a film or TV show, making a scene feel scary, sad or exciting.

Dubbing mixers bring together all the different sounds in the film to create the final mix. When the sound is added to a film, it is called having the **track laid.**

The VFX (visual effects) team combine CGI with real footage to create special effects, such as a tornado ripping through a field, or aliens invading Earth.

DID YOU KNOW?
A green screen allows computer software to separate the body of the actor from the background. It can be used to add a more exciting scene behind the actor.

An actor might have their body scanned and tracked with markers, to be filmed against a green screen, so that animators and **VFX artists** can use computer software to add images to their body and face. This is how most video games are now made.

Animators work with voice recordings of actors to create characters in animated cartoons and movies. They might draw the animations by hand or use computer software or CGI, or a combination of all three!

Colour graders add or change the colour of the people, objects and backgrounds on screen.

A one-hour TV show can take up to six weeks to edit! The **final version** with all of the visual effects, colour grading and sound mix added together is then shown to producers and commissioners. If they're happy with it, the film or show is finished!

WHAT ABOUT THE MORE UNUSUAL FILM AND TV JOBS?

There are many more jobs related to film and TV – here are just a few!

Food stylists make food look perfect for the camera – whether that's a medieval banquet or a slice of pizza eaten on the street!

Set chefs cook all the delicious meals for everyone working on set.

Expert consultants are people who know a lot about a particular subject. This could be a particular time in history, a skill or job, or even exactly what it would be like to live on Mars!

Film and TV reviewers (also known as **critics**) watch films or TV shows before they are released and tell the world what they think about them in newspapers and magazines, and on social media.

If there is dancing in the film, **choreographers** will come up with dances and teach them to actors.

If you love animals, then you could become an **animal wrangler.** They train and care for animals on set.

Drone camera operators are skilled pilots who mount cameras onto drones to film high up in the sky or alongside fast-moving objects such as cars.

The **sales and distribution department** organise the release of the film in cinemas and the TV show on screen.

The **marketing and publicity teams** build a buzz around the film or show in the run-up to its release. They organise interviews with actors, schedule the release of adverts and plan the first screening, known as the premiere – this is when the whole cast and crew can finally celebrate their work!

GET INVOLVED!

If you would like to learn more about being an actor or
working in the film and TV industry, there are many things you can do...

Why not take part in your school play or local theatre production and try out
lots of different jobs, from costume and set design, to directing,
promoting or acting in the production.

You can also join a drama club to learn more about acting, create your
own short film with your friends, practise doing other people's hair
and make-up, pick up a musical instrument and write a script.

To start with, all you need is passion and determination!

USEFUL ORGANISATIONS AND WEBSITES INCLUDE:

Into Film www.intofilm.org/news-and-views/articles/activities-for-young-people-to-do-at-home
BBC Bitesize www.bbc.co.uk/bitesize/topics/z7btrmn/articles/zpkts82#zbm3cxs
National Geographic Kids www.natgeokids.com/uk/discover/science/nature/hamza-yassin-interview
The Lyceum Theatre www.thelyceumtheatre.com/shows/disneys-the-lion-king